Write Something
a course in creative writing for kids

created by Brittany Hampton Tokar
and Jonathan Hampton

illustrated by
Aaron Stewart Lewis Knapp

Classical Violets Publishing
classicalviolets.com

Dear Grown-up,

If you want a child to excel in creative writing, then encourage that child to *be* a creative writer. That probably sounds obvious, but I can't stress enough how important it is for young writers to often be given the freedom to use a blank piece of paper to create their own rules, their own story, their own work of art.

I don't dismiss structure in creative writing education. I appreciate the utility of intriguing and inspiring writing exercises. I've taught courses centered around them, but what I'm against is never encouraging children to just sit down with nothing but a pencil, paper, and one small point of inspiration. What would happen if they were then allowed to simply write, doodle, think, imagine, escape, and create whatever they wish? Give a child permission to sit and stare out a window or look at this workbook or a blank piece of paper for whatever length of time they require, whether it be one minute or one hour. Use the prompts and illustrations in this book in a way that works for your young writer; they provide opportunities for a child to ponder for a while. They are tools to stimulate the young writer's mind. Allow that process to develop naturally and don't rush a little creative writer; thinking is the most important part of writing creatively!

Once a child begins working with this book, try not to give her or him boundaries. Let them think and write whatever comes to their minds, however it comes to their minds. (Even if every single, little thing she writes is about a castle, and everything he writes begins with the same sentence, though it may drive you a bit crazy, just let it be.) You're not looking for perfection here or for something that interests you or sounds good to you. What we want to see as we encourage children to write creatively is something of his or her own.

Some kids may pick up this text and begin their own novels, some may just doodle or list words, and others may feel that writing is a struggle, and all those outcomes are okay here. Because we're not trying to get them to check boxes or complete tasks in a timely manner or write anything in particular. There will be time for those things elsewhere. We're simply asking them to think, feel, wonder, and hopefully, get something original - something truly creative - down on paper.

With hopes for a great learning experience for you and your student,

Brittany

Please read this to or with your child, or have them read it to himself/herself:

Dear Writer,

Have fun with this notebook. Don't worry about being perfect or neat here, unless you love to be perfect and neat. On these pages you should write the way you love to write. Lots of words or a few words. Rhyming words or words that sound completely different next to each other. Tell a fairy tale, or tell about true things. Mix up the truth and fantasy if you like. Write a letter, write about a character you know, or create a character of your own. Just write something. The choices are endless!

In this book you will find questions and ideas and pictures. (Think of the words and images in this book as a place for your mind to start.) Take your time with the ideas and pictures and follow your imagination. And then, when you're ready, pick up your pencil and write something, whatever comes to you. This is creative writing, so be creative. Put something new down on the page, something you think up all on your own. There are no right or wrong answers, no exact way to do this. Your work here is to create something with words, anything you wish.

With hopes for fantastic creations,

Brittany

1. Find a spot you like for writing. Some people like to write at a table or desk, others might sit on the floor and lean up against a wall in a cozy corner, and then there are those who like to write outside, maybe under a favorite tree. Choose a writing spot that makes you feel good and happy, but also makes sense for working with this book and a pencil. Think about the colors around you, the things around you. If you have a favorite picture or pillow, then you might want to have those things nearby. Get comfortable before you write!

2. You've found your spot for writing. Now look around you. Take a slow, deep breath and let it go.

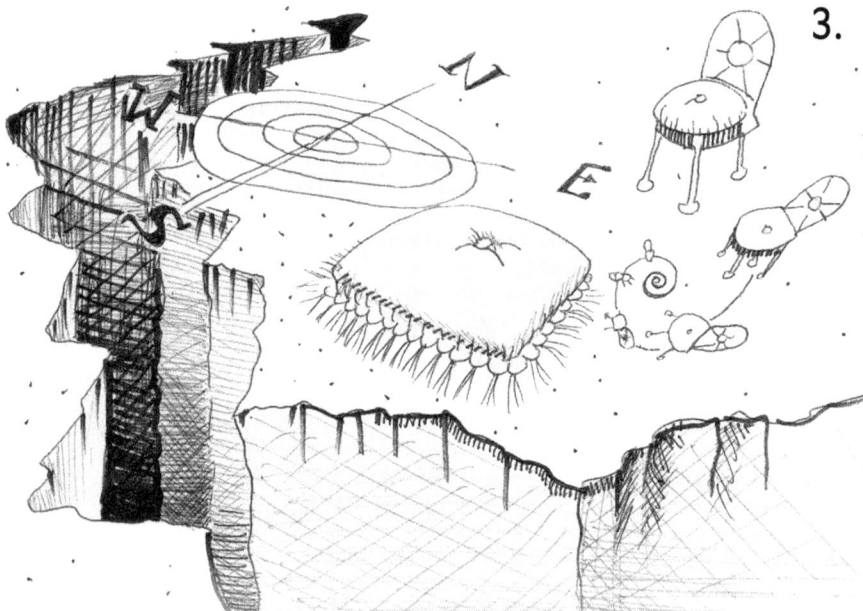

3. Write something. Anything you want! Write whatever comes into your mind. You can write a few lines or you can fill up the following pages. It's up to you!

(This is more space to write something!)

(This is more space to write something!)

1. Think about your favorite storybook.

2. Imagine you are a character in the book.

3. Write something. (Remember, it doesn't matter what you write or how you write it. Just write whatever is in your mind after thinking about yourself being in your favorite storybook. Getting to create anything you can imagine is pretty fun, right?)

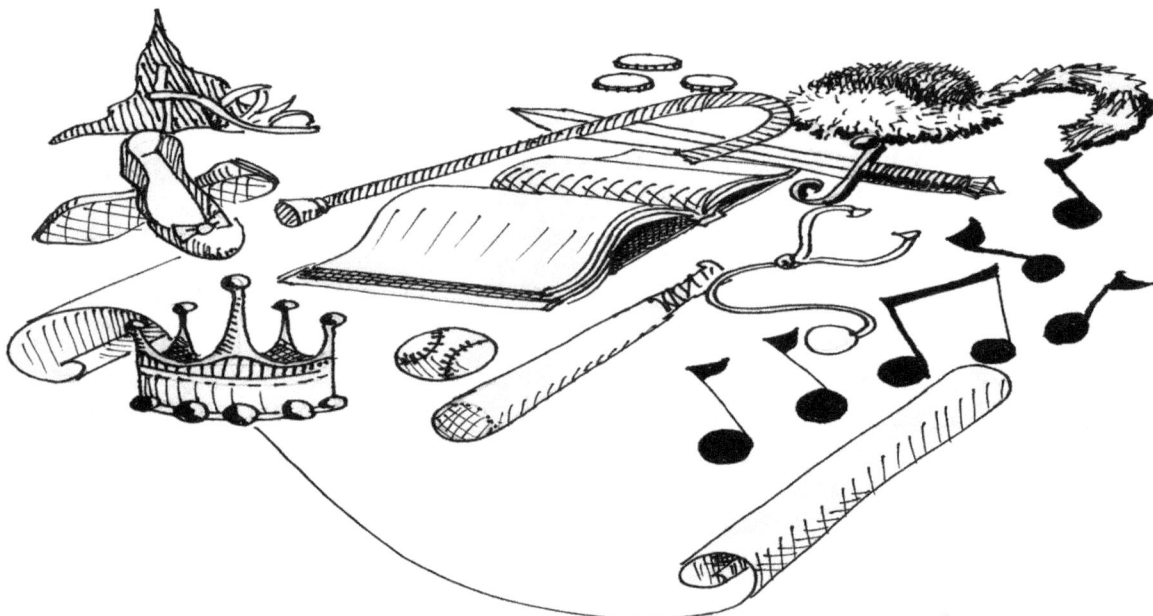

(This is more space to write something!)

(This is more space to write something!)

1. Look at the image below.

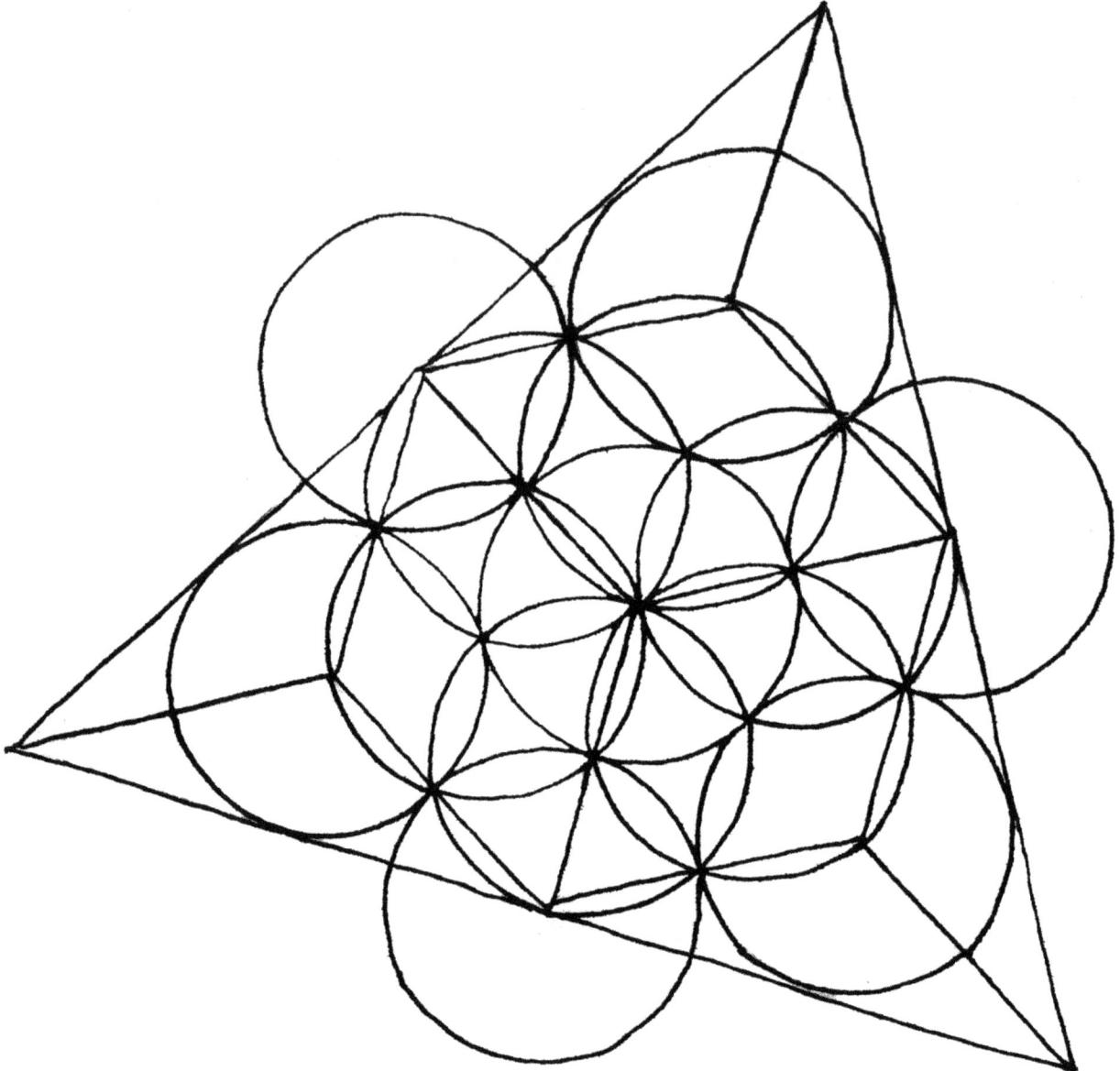

2. Think about whatever pops into your head while you are looking at it. Maybe you would like to relax and let you thoughts go for a while. And then ...

3. Write something. (It's your creation, so write anything you want.)

(This is more space to write something!)

(This is more space to write something!)

1. Think about a good friend.

2. Imagine you and that good friend are going on a secret adventure.

3. Write something. (Hmmm.....are you going to write about that adventure or about something else? It is up to you!)

(This is more space to write something!)

(This is more space to write something!)

1. Pretend someone is making all your favorite foods. Now close your eyes.

2. Think about what you smell around you.

3. Write something. (Did you know that when this book tells you to write something, you can write a story or a list or a poem or a few words that just sound silly or nice together, or you could write a letter or a song or ... or ... or ... anything?!)

(This is more space to write something!)

(This is more space to write something!)

1. Look at the image below.

2. Imagine that you are somewhere trapped inside the image.

3. Write something.

(Anything you want!)

(This is more space to write something!)

(This is more space to write something!)

1. Ask the grown-up with you now if you can go for a walk. This could be a long walk outside or even a small-little-silly walk around your room.

2. Sit back down at your comfy, cozy writing spot. Think about what you saw and heard and felt and smelled on your walk, and think about where your mind wandered.

3. Write something! Remember, you can write anything you want. It's up to you!

(This is more space to write something!)

(This is more space to write something!)

1. Remember that walk you took for the writing time before this one? Think about that walk. It might help to close your eyes and think. Sometimes your mind can work more clearly if your eyes are closed.

2. Now think about what you did *not* see on the walk.

3. Write something. (Something?....yep, any something *you* want. You are the writer, the author, the artist, the one in charge of the blank page. This is *your* book!)

(This is more space to write something!)

(This is more space to write something!)

1. Imagine that you are a famous explorer. Now, imagine you are a movie star. Now, imagine you are a great inventor. And after that, imagine you have your very own ice cream shop with 584 flavors of ice cream.

2. Think about all of the spectacular things you can do in your life. If you aren't sure yet what "spectacular" means, then ask the grown-up around you. (It's a pretty great word, so it is worth a minute to learn it.) Keep thinking about all of those spectacular things you can do, and then ...

3. Write something. You can write about anything you want!

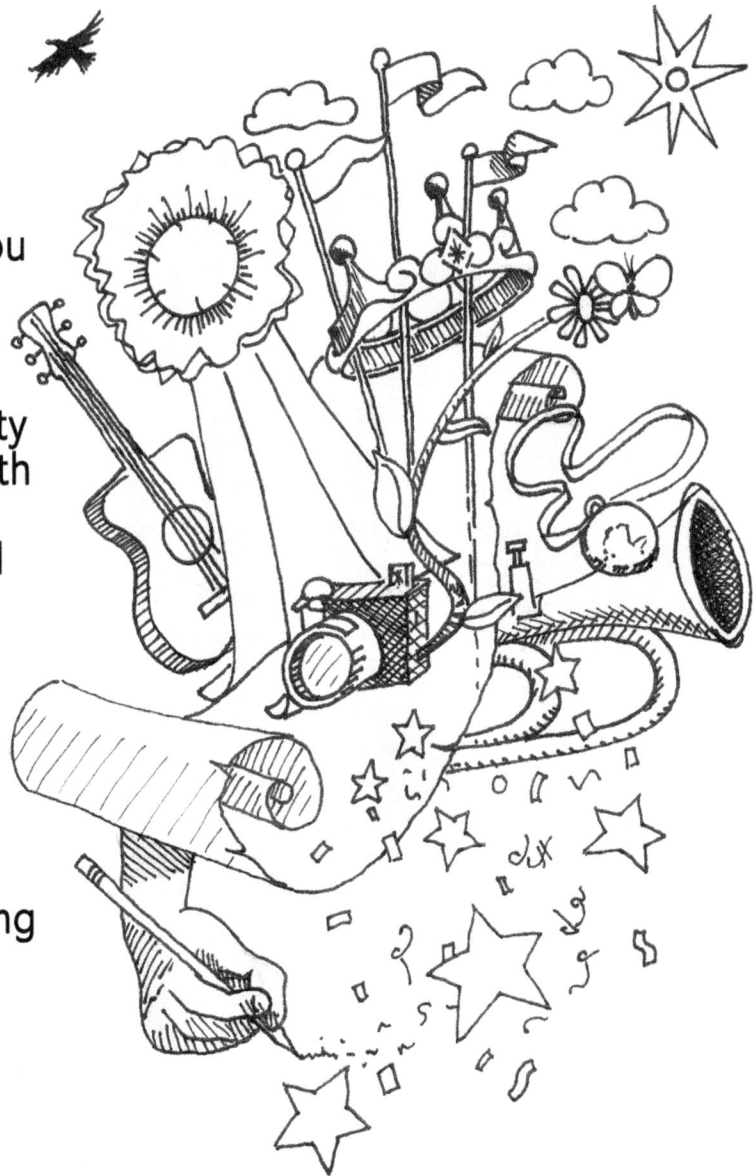

(This is more space to write something!)

(This is more space to write something!)

1. Think of some words that rhyme. I'll start: big, wig, fig, jig. Now, it's your turn.

2. Say those rhyming words over and over until they get all twisted up together in your mouth.

3. Write something. (Will you write something that rhymes, or will you run away from those rhyming words and write something totally different? It is up to you, because you are the writer!)

(This is more space to write something!)

(This is more space to write something!)

SAP   BLUE

1. Find something near you that is the color green.

2. Look at that green thing. What other things does the green thing make you think of?

3. Now write something. (Be creative! Write anything you want. Maybe you will write about the green thing you found or the things it made you think of. Or, maybe you will write about something completely different, something not green at all, maybe something yellow, or blue, or even invisible. It's up to you!)

Fern   Teal   Pine

Lime   Sea   AQUA   Viridian

LIGHT   GRASS   FOREST   ALGAE

HUNTERS   Olive   Spring   Slime   yellow

(This is more space to write something!)

(This is more space to write something!)

1. Think about your favorite season. Is it winter, spring, summer, or autumn?

2. Make a list in your head of reasons why that season is your favorite.

3. Now (you guessed it!) write something. Will you write a story set in your favorite season? Are you going to write about a snowman in a winter storm; a perfectly purple flower in spring; a sandbox full of fresh, sparkling sand in summer; a big maple tree with bright golden leaves in fall? Or, maybe you will write about something that doesn't have anything at all to do with your favorite season. Hmmm ... what will you write? I wonder...

(This is more space to write something!)

(This is more space to write something!)

1. Think about something that moves very fast.

2. Now imagine that the very fast something gets stuck in the mud.

3. Write something. A poem about mud, a letter to a friend who runs really fast, or maybe you'll write a song about getting stuck in the mud while riding a bicycle lickety-split. Or maybe you'll write something completely different ...

(This is more space to write something!)

(This is more space to write something!)

1. Look at the image below.

2. Imagine you are swimming around inside this image.

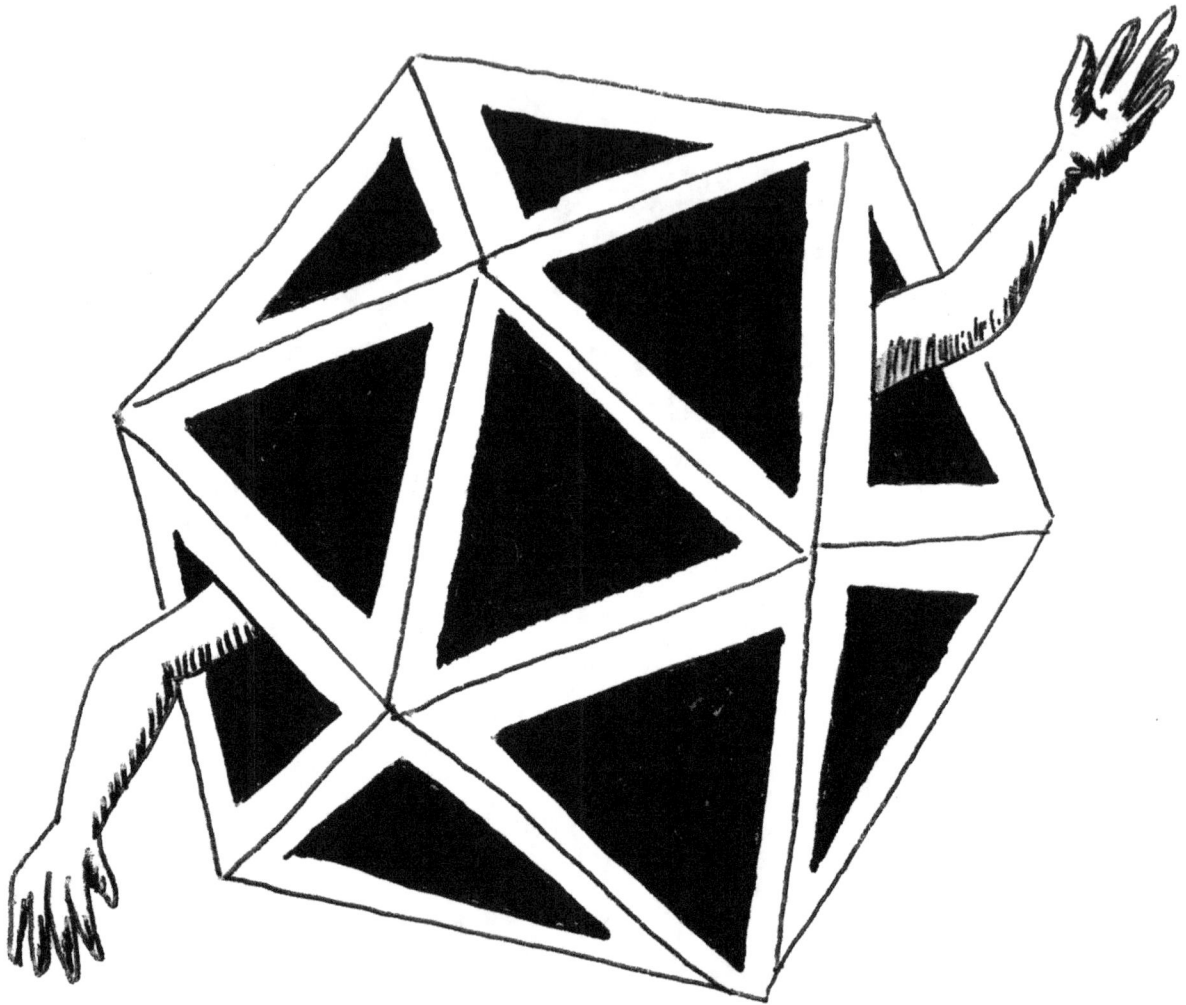

3. Write something. I wonder if you will write a list of things you see and feel inside the image. Or maybe you will forget about this image altogether and write a song. It doesn't matter if you write about this image or not. This is your page. Just write something. Anything.

(This is more space to write something!)

(This is more space to write something!)

1. Sing a song. Sing any song you wish. Create a new song to sing, if you want.

2. Now try to sing that song backwards. That's difficult to do, isn't it? And maybe a little silly ... singing songs backwards ... how funny ...

3. Now guess what I'm going to ask you to do? Write something - whatever you want to create!

(This is more space to write something!)

(This is more space to write something!)

1. Write your name somewhere on this page.

2. Say your name out loud. Say it slowly and think about the different sounds in your name. Whisper your name a few times. Look at the letters in your name. Think about the way the letters are shaped and how they look together. How do you feel when you look at your name? What does your name mean? Do you know other people with your name? What is the best part of your name? Think about your name and what it means to you.

3. Write something. Anything you want!

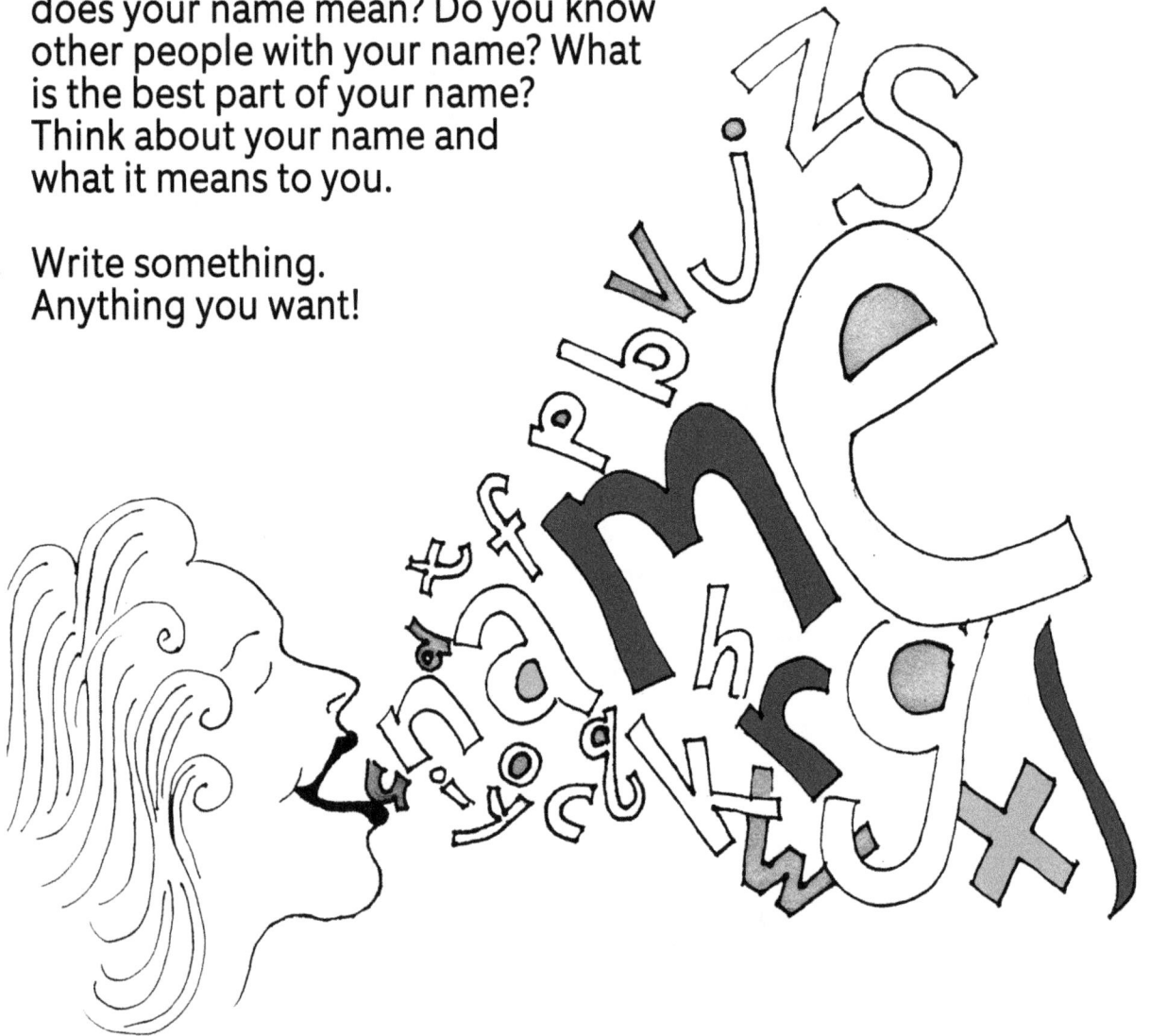

(This is more space to write something!)

(This is more space to write something!)

1. Close your eyes and think about something that smells wonderful. Take some slow breaths in through your nose and pretend that you can smell the wonderful smell. Can you almost smell it in your mind?

2. Open your eyes and keep on thinking about that wonderful smell and how it makes you feel. And now ...

3. Write something. Anything!

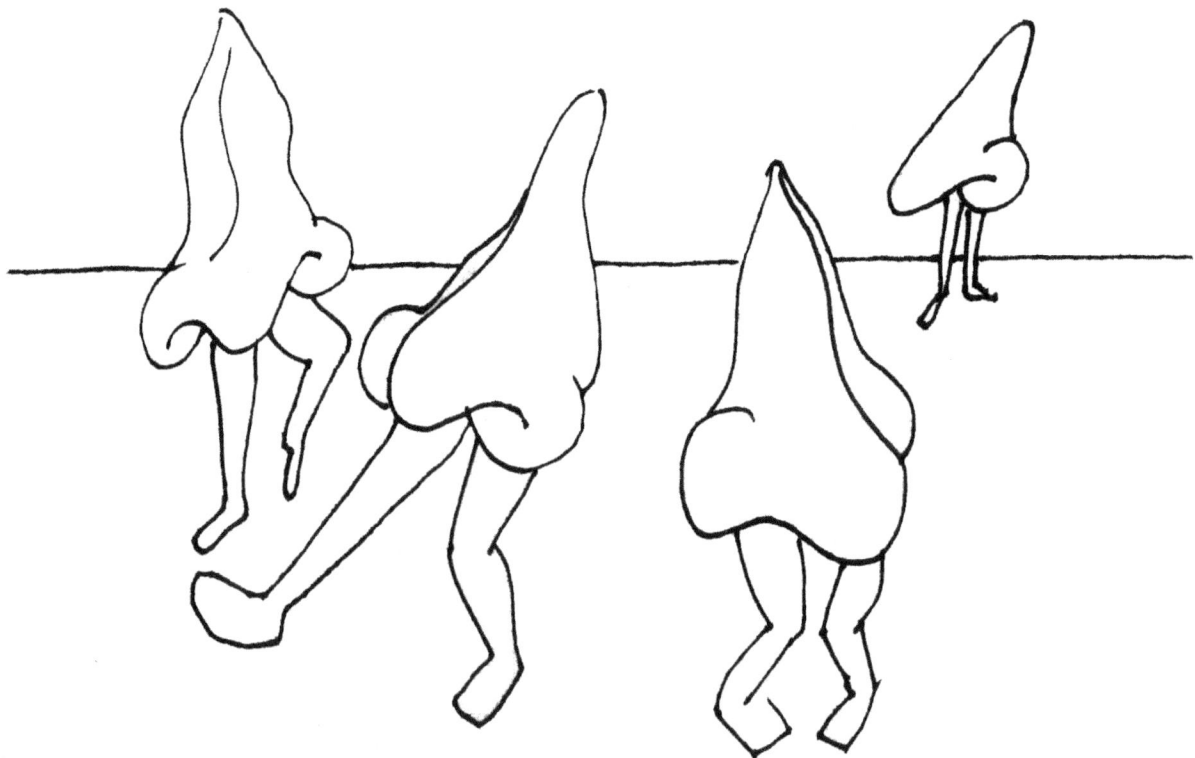

(This is more space to write something!)

(This is more space to write something!)

1. Think about a really loud-sounding noise. What is the loudest sound you have ever heard? What is something in your imagination that you know would be really, really loud?

2. Close your eyes and pretend you are listening to that really loud-sounding noise. Imagine that the noise stops and it becomes silent, as silent as a forest at nighttime when there is snow on the ground and the animals are sleeping underground and in their hiding places.

3. Now that things have quieted down in your imagination, write something. I wonder what you'll write here ...

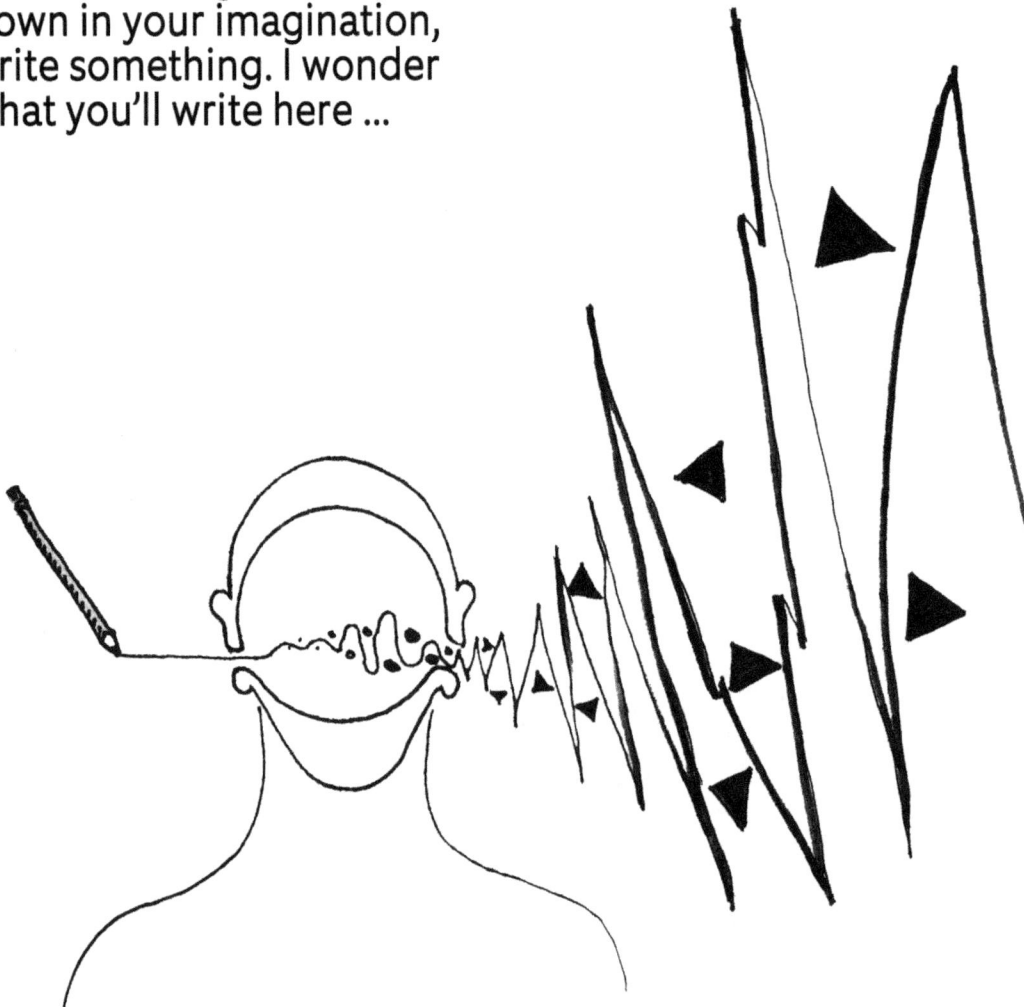

(This is more space to write something!)

(This is more space to write something!)

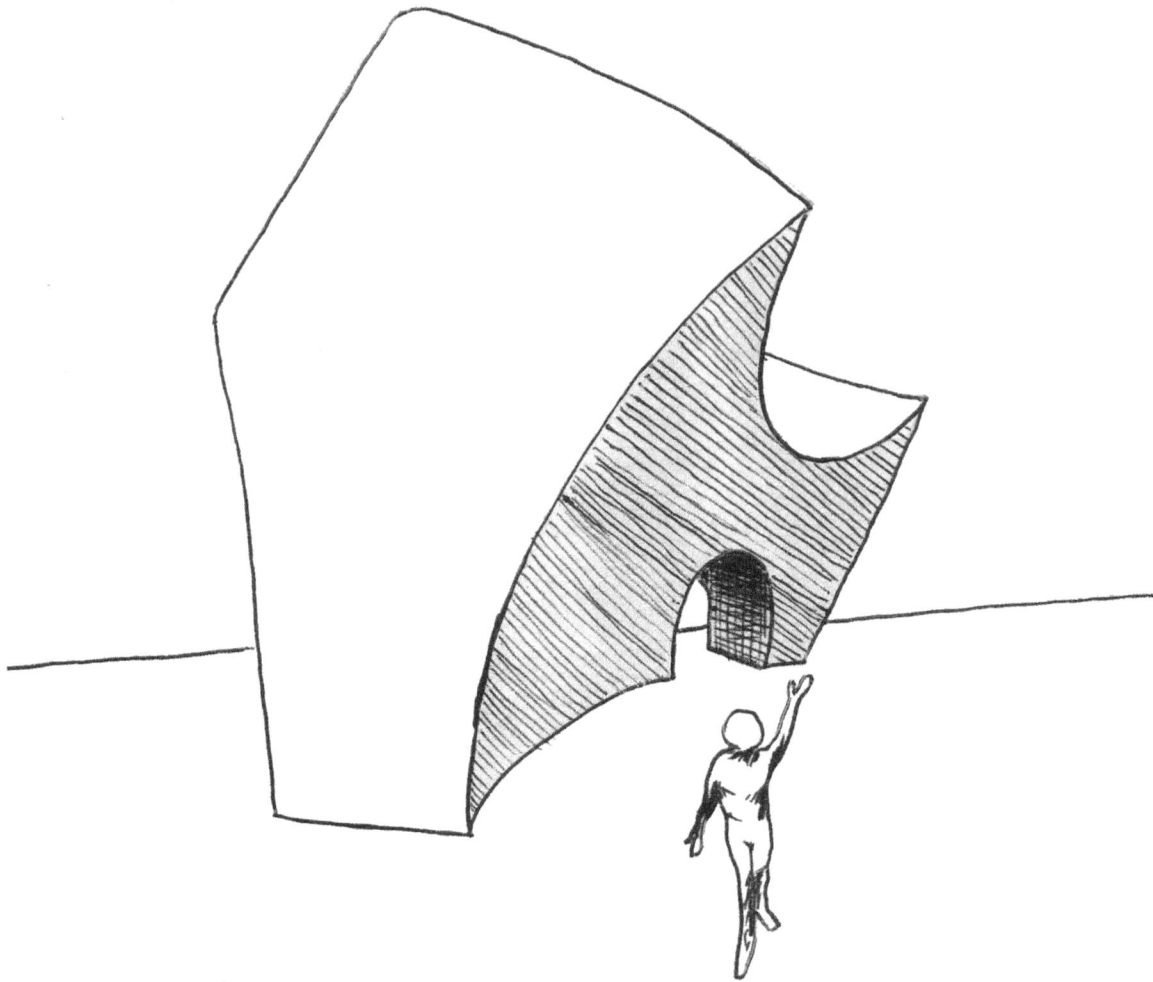

1. Look at the shape above.

2. Pretend you are super small and are standing in the shade of this
    shape. What does it feel like standing beside a great, big shape
    that is much larger than you? Keep on thinking about being next
    to the shape for a few more moments, and then ...

3. Write something! (Remember, you are the creator here; you can
    write about anything you want.)

(This is more space to write something!)

(This is more space to write something!)

1. Imagine that you are the author of a series of children's books. Who are the characters in your book? What can they do and where will they go and what will they see when they get there?

2. Think about the main character of the books you are imagining that you have written. Think about who this character would be. What would his or her or its name be? Would your character be a super-hero, or a not-so-super hero, or no kind of hero at all? Would your character do lots of exciting and adventurous things, or would he or she be timid and stay close to home? What kind of snacks would your character like? Think and think and then think some more about the character in your imaginary series of books.

3. And then when you have thought so much about the character that you feel like you really know this person, write something. Write something about this character, or take a break from this character and chase a new idea that comes to mind. Write whatever you want.

(This is more space to write something!)

(This is more space to write something!)

1. Touch this piece of paper in your workbook. Touch the page with a single finger, and then with your whole hand. Touch the picture and these words.

2. What words come to mind when you touch the paper? Pick at least three such words. You can write them in the blanks below, and then ...

3. Write something. Remember, you can create any kind of writing that you want!

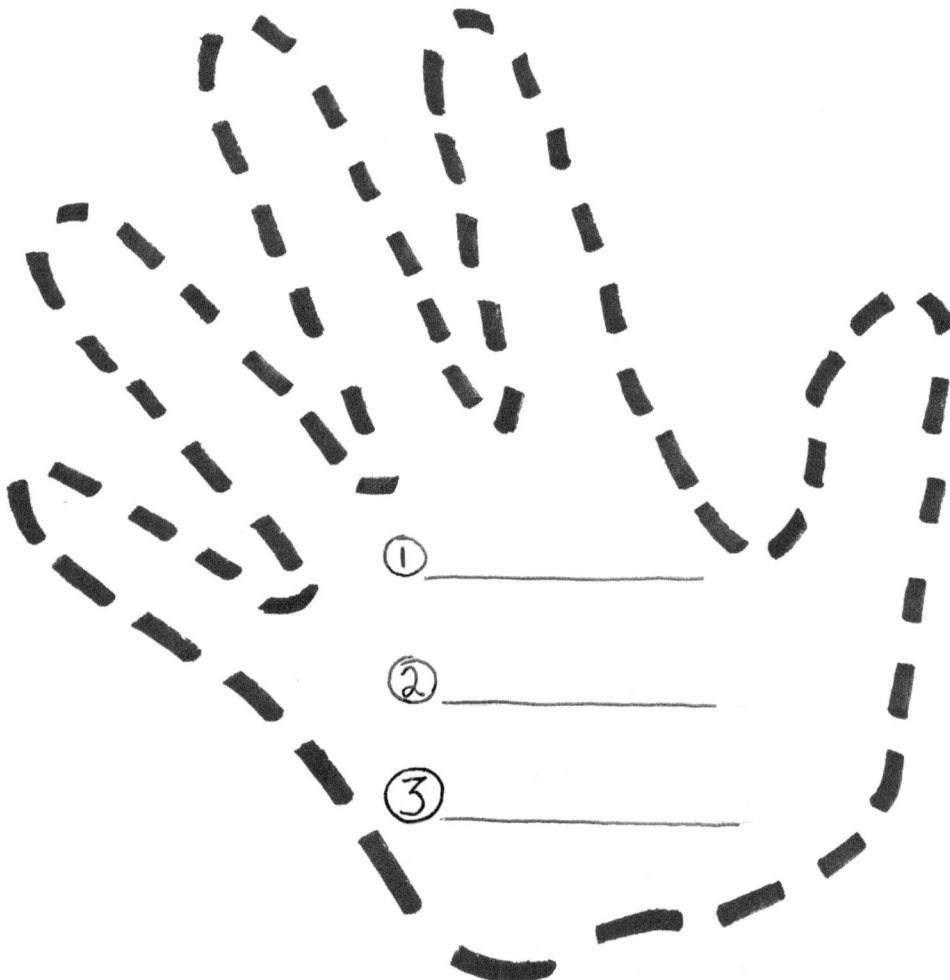

① _____

② _____

③ _____

(This is more space to write something!)

(This is more space to write something!)

1. Pick up your pencil.

2. Now drop it on the ground. What kind of sound did it make? Drop it again if you didn't catch the sound well the first time. Can you recreate the sound with your voice? Was the sound quick or sharp or hard or soft or short or funny or non-existent or unexpected or beautiful or dull or what?

3. After you decide what the pencil hitting the floor sounded like, write something. Write something only you could write. Anything that comes to your phenomenal mind. Anything at all.

(This is more space to write something!)

(This is more space to write something!)

1. Imagine you are a famous painter.

2. Now close your eyes. Imagine something you might like to paint. What would that painting look like? How might you explain your painting to a friend? What words could describe your fabulous painting?

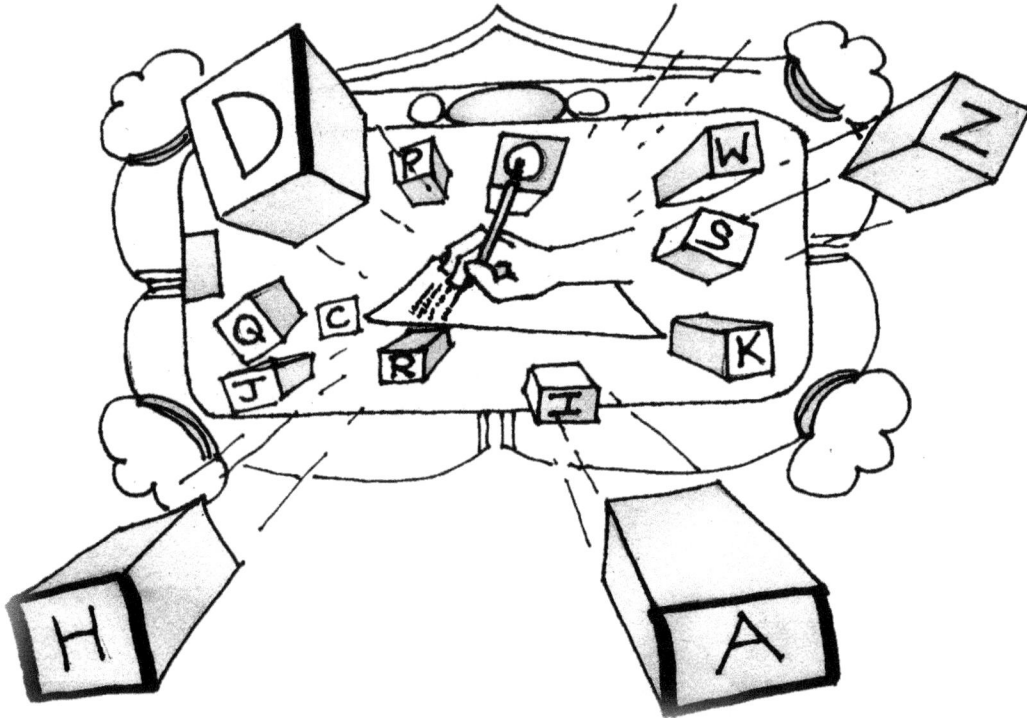

3. Once you have described your fabulous painting in your head, go ahead and writing something down on the following page or pages. Will you write about what your imaginary painting would look like? Or will you write a story about what is happening in the scene of your painting? Or will you write about how creating art makes you feel? Or will you write about something that has nothing at all to do with pretending you are a famous painter with a fabulous painting. Maybe you will write about horses and ice hockey. Just, please, if you will, young author, write something!

(This is more space to write something!)

(This is more space to write something!)

1. Look at the image below.

2. If this image made a sound, what would it be? If this picture had a smell, what would it smell like? If this thing just appeared in your room out of nowhere, what would you do? If you had to describe this thing in three words, what would they be?

3. And now, write something. You could write about a smell or a feeling or the place where this image belongs or about a wonderful thought that is all your own.

(This is more space to write something!)

(This is more space to write something!)

1. Think about a really great gift you would like to receive.

2. Now close your eyes and imagine yourself receiving that really great gift from someone you really like. And as you imagine this, smile really big. Think about how you feel as you imagine this really great gift and as you smile a really big smile. Is there an amazing gift that you want to give someone else?

3. After you've had that wonderful imagining smile, write something. And remember, you are the writer, the author, the word artist, so let yourself write whatever comes to you or whatever you feel like writing.

(This is more space to write something!)

(This is more space to write something!)

1. Imagine you've worked really hard and completed a whole book of your own writing from your own imagination.

2. Think about what it would feel like to hold a completed workbook in your hands, one that is full of your own creative writing. Would you feel happy or relieved or excited or tired or full of energy? How would you feel about that?

3. Once you've thought about that, write something. Write anything you want.

(This is more space to write something!)

(This is more space to write something!)